ABBOTSFORD, ROXBURGHSHIRE

In 1811, Sir Walter Scott spent 4,000 guineas on a small farm called Cartleyhole on the bank of the River Tweed. As the land formerly belonged to the monks of Melrose, Sir Walter decided on a more romantic and fitting name: Abbotsford. It was here that he wrote the highly popular Waverley novels, and with success came the desire for a grander house and more land, the result of which can be seen today.

Following Sir Walter's death in 1832, tourists, including Queen Victoria, visited Abbotsford in great numbers. Attractions include his study, largely unchanged, and his library of 20,000 books. Apart from his literary legacy, Scott's study of Scottish history led to the discovery of the Scottish regalia – the Crown, Sceptre and Sword of State – in an old chest in Edinburgh Castle, which are now on display there.

◀ BLAIR CASTLE, PERTHSHIRE

For more than seven centuries, Blair Castle has been the home of the Earls and Dukes of Atholl (motto: Furth Fortune and Fill the Fetters). It has undergone much change to its fortunes over the years: from the glory of several royal visitations to the ignominy of occupation; from the ravages of siege to those of fashion. Comyn's (or Cumming's) Tower was built in the 13th century. Mary Queen of Scots was entertained to a hunt at the castle in the 16th century. Cromwell's troops paid an unwelcome visit during the Civil War and it was again under siege during the Jacobite rebellion – the last private castle in Britain to be besieged. The castle had been remodelled as a mansion by 1758, only to be restored to its medieval appearance a century later.

Blair Castle stands in extensive landscaped grounds which include trails and cycle paths for visitors.

▲ BRAEMAR CASTLE, ABERDEENSHIRE

Sixty years after the L-shaped tower house had been built by the Earl of Mar in 1628, Braemar Castle was burned down by a rival clan, the feuding Farquharsons of Invercauld, led by their legendary leader John 'the Black Colonel'. The castle was rebuilt in the mid-18th century to billet English soldiers fresh from their success at the Battle of Culloden. Their occupation was designed to quell any further uprising by the Highland clans. The castle's new defences included the first 'star wars' – a many-angled star-shaped curtain wall through which soldiers could protect as much of the surrounding area as possible. The English left other lasting marks – notably their names scratched in wood – and visitors today can see the old underground pit-prison.

Braemar is famously the setting for the annual games – the Royal Highland Gathering.

CASTLE CAMPBELL, CLACKMANNANSHIRE

Known as Castle Gloom when it was built towards the end of the 15th century, it stood beside Gloomhill, watered by the Burn of Sorrow and the Burn of Care. The first Earl of Argyll changed the name to Castle Campbell by Act of Parliament in 1489. But perhaps he should have renamed it Castle Doom, for Cromwell's supporters torched it in the mid-17th century and its use as a residence ended.

The castle is set in the attractive surroundings of 24 hectares (60 acres) of the Dollar Glen woodland.

CAWDOR CASTLE, NAIRNSHIRE ▶

Cawdor Castle comes complete with moat, drawbridge, arched gateway, brooding central tower with turrets, a dungeon – and massive publicity from William Shakespeare who used it as the murder scene in *Macbeth*. The great tower and older parts of the present castle date from 1454 but much of the structure belongs to the 17th century when Sir Hugh Campbell ordered the fortress to be remodelled.

Notable gardens surround Cawdor Castle, which perches on a rocky bank high above the Cawdor Burn, 8 kilometres (5 miles) from Nairn.

CULZEAN CASTLE, AYRSHIRE

Though built after castles ceased to be needed to protect inhabitants from attack, rich romantics continued to create impressive structures styled and called after their fortress forerunners. Culzean Castle (pronounced Cullain) is considered one of the triumphs of Robert Adam, Scotland's most illustrious architect. Built for the 10th Earl of Cassillis in the 1780s, it stands on a cliff top overlooking the Firth of Clyde on a site occupied by the Kennedy family from the 14th century.

Culzean contains a flat put at the disposal of General Eisenhower, Supreme Commander of the Allied Forces in Europe, at the end of the Second World War.

The extensive country park grounds include a swan pond, deer park and woods.

◄ DUNFERMLINE ABBEY, DUNFERMLINE

The great Benedictine abbey rises from a modest 11th-century church, founded by Queen Margaret, which can be seen beneath the abbey nave. A shrine to St Margaret was erected in the 13th century, but the most famous memorial is to King Robert the Bruce, 14th-century hero of the medieval Wars of Independence, Scotland's struggle against England. Bruce was buried in the choir; the site of his tomb is marked with a modern brass in the church built on the site of the abbey.

The remains of the monastery's domestic buildings can be seen today. It was a boastful claim, made proudly in the 13th century, that 'two distinguished sovereigns with their retinues might be accommodated at the same time without inconvenience to one another'.

NEW TOWN, EDINBURGH

▲

A determined civic leader, Lord Provost Drummond, and a talented young architect, James Craig, were responsible for the inspired and elegant development of Edinburgh which started in the 18th century: New Town.

The stylish new development expanded and rapidly attracted the rich and refined. George Street links two elegant squares – St Andrew and Charlotte, a symbol of the union between Scotland and England after centuries of war and struggle. St Andrew Square, home to numerous bank and insurance company offices, is said to be the richest square in Europe. Charlotte Square is regarded as an architectural gem set with the green-domed St George's kirk.

The Moray Estate, built on the Earl of Moray's estate in the 1820s, was designed by James Gillespie Graham and is an architectural delight, with sweeping crescents and circuses joined by short avenues.

Edinburgh's main thoroughfare, Princes Street, is one of the most magnificent shopping streets in Europe. It is remarkable in having shops on only one side, providing a spectacular and uninterrupted view of the castle.

EDINBURGH CASTLE

◀

Perched high on an extinct volcanic outcrop, Edinburgh Castle's origins go back more than 1,400 years. A basic stronghold was converted to a royal castle in the 11th century. St Margaret's Chapel within the castle walls is now Edinburgh's oldest surviving building. The main castle buildings (dating from the 16th century) form three sides of a courtyard known as Crown Square. It contains the bedchamber where Mary Queen of Scots gave birth to James VI of Scotland, later crowned King James I of England and thus uniting the two warring countries.

Proudly guarding the gatehouse entrance to the castle are the statues of two of Scotland's greatest heroes – William Wallace and Robert the Bruce.

EILEAN DONAN, ROSS AND CROMARTY

At the point where Lochs Alsh, Long and Duich meet stands the island castle of Eilean Donan, reached by visitors via a causeway. The bleak but sturdy structure, lapped by the waters and backed by distant hills, is one of the most evocative sights of Scotland. Dating back to the 13th century, much of the castle was ruined in the 18th century by the English. It was restored in the 20th century by Colonel MacRae-Gilstrap and incorporates a memorial to the Clan MacRae.

◄ PALACE OF HOLYROODHOUSE, EDINBURGH

When Her Majesty The Queen is in Scotland, the Palace of Holyroodhouse is her official residence. But the palace is most closely associated with Scotland's most tragic monarch, Mary Queen of Scots.

The palace started as a guest house for the abbey, founded in the 12th century by King David I. As the abbey slowly slid into decay over the centuries, the palace rose by its side. The jealous husband of Mary Queen of Scots murdered her secretary, Rizzio, here in the 16th century. Following a fire in the 17th century, King Charles II had the palace rebuilt in the style seen today. The oldest parts include King James Tower, which contains the rooms of Mary Queen of Scots.

The picture gallery houses portraits – though not authentic – of more than a hundred Scottish monarchs.

FALKLAND PALACE, FIFE

An old fortress has stood on this site since the 12th century. The Royal Palace dates from the 15th century, when it was used as a royal hunting lodge. Here the Stewart kings and queens came to relax by practising their archery skills, playing tennis, riding and hawking. King James II started the major alterations that transformed Falkland into a Renaissance palace. Kings James IV and V later enlarged and embellished it. The massive twin-turretted gatehouse, which carries the coat of arms of Stuart of Bute, was part of James V's plans. Falkland Palace was lived in by Mary Queen of Scots and her son, King James VI/I. It was visited by Charles I, and from here Charles II left Falkland for defeat and exile.

FLOORS CASTLE, ROXBURGHSHIRE

Built between 1718 and 1740, for many years it was thought that Floors Castle was designed by Sir John Vanbrugh. However, it is now known that William Adam was both architect and builder, and it was later embellished by William Playfair. Home of the Dukes of Roxburghe, Floors is described as the largest inhabited mansion in Britain but has retained its feeling of a comfortable residence rather than a museum.

French prisoners from the Napoleonic wars built part of the wall round the castle which extends to 22,250 hectares (55,000 acres). In the grounds is a holly tree believed to mark the spot where King James II was mortally wounded by an exploding cannon at the siege of Roxburghe in 1460.

FORTH BRIDGES, WEST LOTHIAN

The Forth Rail Bridge, linking Fife to Edinburgh, was built over a century ago. For generations it has represented one of the greatest engineering feats in the world. The total length of the bridge, including approach roads, is some $2\frac{1}{2}$ kilometres ($1\frac{1}{2}$ miles) and it took 5,000 men to build it.

The road bridge is one of the world's longest suspension bridges, which took six years to complete. Its two main towers rise over 150 metres (500 feet) above the Forth. The bridge was opened by Her Majesty Queen Elizabeth II in 1964.

◀ FORT AUGUSTUS, INVERNESS-SHIRE

A fort was erected at the southern end of Loch Ness in the 18th century. It was named after William Augustus, Duke of Cumberland, who was famed and feared for his savagery in putting down the rebellion at the Battle of Culloden. The fort became his headquarters in the aftermath of the battle.

Although no longer occupied by monks, the old fort was converted to a Benedictine abbey over a century ago.

GLAMIS CASTLE, ANGUS

Glamis (pronounced Glahms) is closely associated with the Royal Family, being the birthplace of Her Majesty The Queen's sister, Princess Margaret, and the childhood home of their mother.

The castle is the family home of the Earls of Strathmore and Kinghorne and has been a royal residence since the 14th century. It is also the legendary setting of Shakespeare's *Macbeth*. Malcolm II died here (probably violently) in the 11th century and Lady Glamis was burned for witchcraft in the 16th century. Visitors today can see a notable collection of paintings, tapestries and furniture, as well as a park which was landscaped towards the end of the 18th century.

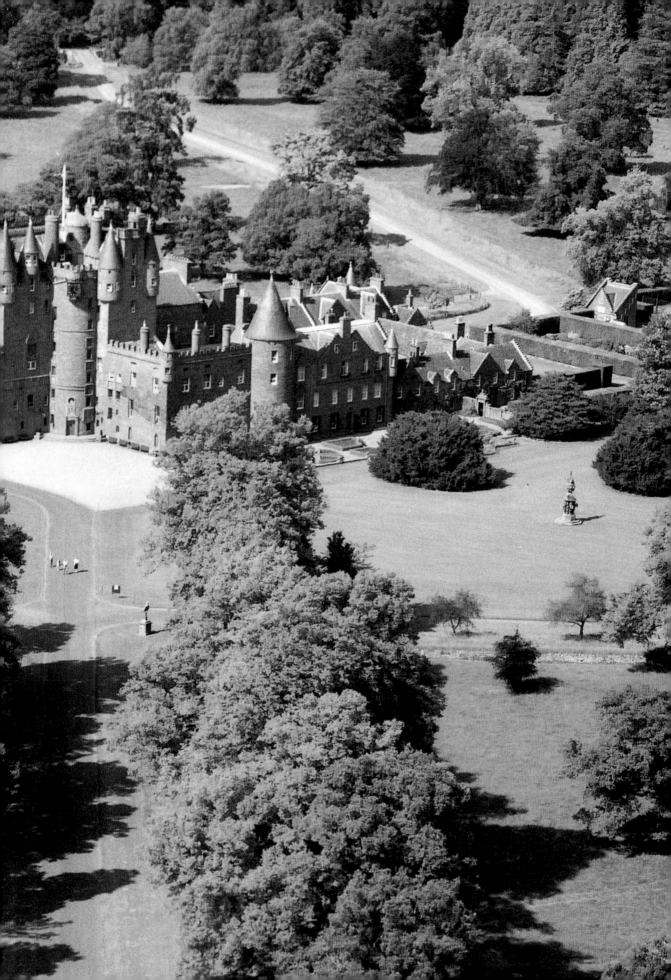

GLASGOW

While London has Trafalgar Square, Glasgow's most famous focal point is George Square. Laid out in the 18th century and named after King George III, it was later enhanced by the 24-metre (80-foot) high Doric column topped by a statue of Edinburgh novelist Sir Walter Scott. Around the column are statues of Scottish heroes, including Burns, Watt and Livingstone. The Renaissance-style City Chambers were added to the Square in the late 19th century. The Banqueting Hall displays murals showing Glasgow's progress.

Scotland's second city has recently achieved status as a centre for cultural excellence. Its Art Gallery and Museum has arguably the finest municipal art collection in the UK and the Burrell Collection in Pollok Country Park is a showcase for nearly 9,000 works of art.

GLEN COE, ARGYLL

Combining dramatic mountain scenery with memories of an historical massacre, much of Glen Coe is protected by The National Trust for Scotland. Features include the Study, a rocky spot which gives the celebrated view of the hills known as the Three Sisters of Glen Coe. Signal Rock is where the signal for the start of the massacre in 1692 was given; some 40 local people of the Macdonald clan were killed and their homes razed. A monument to the fallen Macdonalds is situated on the road to Invercoe.

▲ THE GREAT GLEN, INVERNESS-SHIRE

Known geologically as a natural fissure, scoured by glaciers during the last ice age, the real name of this outstanding feature is Glen Mohr Albin, but its popular name – the Great Glen – more accurately describes it. Stretching some 96 kilometres (60 miles) from Inverness in the north east to Fort William in the south west, the Great Glen is made up of four lochs – Loch Ness, Loch Dochfour, Loch Oich and Loch Lochy – linked by the unique waterway known as the Caledonian Canal.

A road built by General Wade once traversed the glen from end to end, but today's road only partly follows the route.

INVERARAY CASTLE, ARGYLL ▶

Seat of the Dukes of Argyll, Inveraray Castle is one of Western Scotland's jewels. Standing in wooded parkland, the baronial-style mansion dates from the 1700s, built to replace an earlier 16th-century structure. Much of the old town of Inveraray was demolished to make way for the present building. The task of constructing the new burgh and castle was given to a London architect, Roger Morris, and the famous Adam family. The castle's magnificent interior decoration features Adam chimney pieces, ancient arms, works of art, and relics of the Dukes of Argyll, chiefs of Clan Campbell.

INVERNESS, INVERNESS-SHIRE

Situated on the mouth of the River Ness, Inverness is known as 'Capital of the Highlands'. King Brude ruled the region from here in the 6th century. Fortifications at Inverness have developed from a wooden castle (on Auld Castle Hill) to a stone castle which was subsequently strengthened. Inverness has been the target of attack throughout history: in the 11th century by Malcolm Canmore to avenge the death of his father; several times during the Scottish War of Independence; during the 18th-century Jacobite rebellions; and when Mary Queen of Scots was refused entry to the castle, clans loyal to her attacked it and hanged the Governor for treason.

The present castle structure dates from the 19th century.

KILCHURN CASTLE, ARGYLL ▶

Originally Macgregor territory, this proud baronial stronghold became the principal residence of the Campbells of Glenorchy, later the Earls and Marquis of Breadalbane. Standing on a rocky spit, once an island, it overlooks Loch Awe which stretches for some 37 kilometres (23 miles).

Kilchurn's keep dates back to the 15th century, but the north and south sides were added in the late 17th century. Half a century later, it was taken by Hanoverian troops. The destructive gale of 1879 which brought down the Tay railway bridge also toppled one of Kilchurn Castle's towers. The ruin's setting, with Ben Cruachan as a backdrop, is a celebrated sight in this corner of Argyll.

◄ LINLITHGOW PALACE, WEST LOTHIAN

A royal residence has been at Linlithgow, overlooking the loch, since the 12th century. Through the centuries, Linlithgow's fortunes have reflected the state of the English/Scottish struggle for power. The present palace was begun in the 15th century. King James V and later Mary Queen of Scots were born here; Scottish parliaments were held here. But with the eventual 1707 union between Scotland and England, Linlithgow was left to sink slowly into decay.

St Michael's Church stands in the palace's shadow, although its origins pre-date even the palace. Whilst at his devotions in St Katherine's aisle, King James IV is said to have received a ghostly prophecy of his impending disaster on the battlefield of Flodden.

▲ LOCH LEVEN, KINROSS-SHIRE

On an island on Loch Leven stands the squat 14th-century castle with 16th century tower which knew its finest hour in the reign of Mary Queen of Scots.

Mary was taken here in 1567 and imprisoned for nearly a year. Although her own supporters tried to rescue her, an 18-year-old member of the Douglas family (who were acting as her gaoler) helped her escape. William Douglas secretly took the keys, carefully unlocked the queen and relocked the castle to allay suspicion, then rowed her safely ashore.

A century later, Kinross House was built on the mainland facing the castle. It was designed by architect Sir William Bruce in classically elegant Palladian style, with magnificent formal gardens which echo the symmetry of the house.

LOCH LOMOND, STIRLINGSHIRE/DUMBARTONSHIRE

Britain's largest inland stretch of water is 38 kilometres
(24 miles) long and is, in parts, 8 kilometres (5 miles) wide.
The loch is studded with thirty islands, the largest of which
contains the ruins of an old castle. Boating and pleasure steam-
ers ply the area, but the waters also serve a practical purpose –
feeding Scotland's industrial heartland.

PERTH, PERTHSHIRE ▶

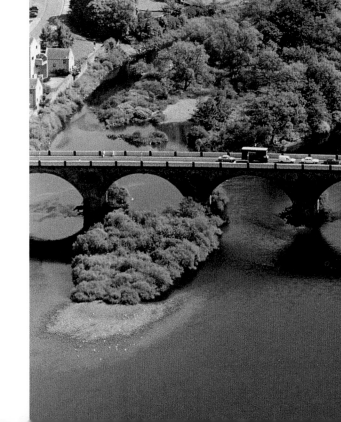

Seven main routes meet at Perth. In ancient times it was the
first possible spot for bridging the River Tay. Its role as a cross-
roads trading place of considerable importance was recorded
by the Romans, though remains of settlements dating back
8,000 years have been found. The Romans built their fort
Bertha at Perth, abandoned in the late 80s AD.

Closely associated with Scone, the ancient coronation site
of Scottish monarchs, Perth became one of the foremost religious centres in the land. The 12th-century Church of St John
was where, in the 16th century, the Protestant John Knox
launched his crusade against papist idolatry with his fire and
brimstone sermon on the 'cleansing of the temple'.

ST ANDREWS, FIFE

The cathedral at St Andrews, begun in the 12th century, was once the largest in Scotland. All that remains are parts of the south wall of the nave, choir, south transept, and east and west doorways. In the 16th century, John Knox's followers attacked the cathedral structure as a result of his 'cleansing of the temple' sermon at Perth's Church of St John.

The castle was founded in 1200 by Bishop Roger and rebuilt in the late 14th century, though the surviving parts seen today largely date from the 16th century. The castle's bloodiest time came in the 16th century during the religious Reformation struggles. Cardinal David Beaton had a Protestant reformer burnt to death for heresy, only to be murdered himself at the castle three months later. The Protestants, with John Knox as their chaplain, were besieged in the castle for a year. During that time, mines were tunnelled through the rocks below.

The University of St Andrews has a global reputation for academic excellence. Founded in 1411, it is the oldest university in Scotland and the third oldest in Britain.

The town is particularly famous for its association with the Royal and Ancient Golf Club of St Andrews and its celebrated status throughout the world as 'the home of golf'.

SCONE PALACE, PERTHSHIRE

An ancient mound at Scone has been the scene of coronations and parliaments and the source of legends for centuries.

King Kenneth I (843–59), who united the Picts and Scots, is credited with bringing to Scone the Sacred Stone of Destiny on which all kings of Scotland were crowned. The Stone's origins are obscure: some believe it is the original 'Jacob's Pillow'; others a pagan altar stone. It was kept here for five centuries until King Edward I made off with it and placed it in Westminster Abbey in the 13th century. Since that time Britain's monarchs – including

Her Majesty Queen Elizabeth II – have been crowned on the Coronation Chair on which the simple slab lay until 1996. The Stone is now housed alongside the Honours of Scotland in Edinburgh Castle, although a replica sits upon the Moot Hill marking the site of the original. The small chapel (inset) standing on the Moot Hill dates from the early 19th century, along with the castellated palace seen today.

Scone Palace has been in the family of the present Earl of Mansfield for nearly 400 years.

◀ STIRLING CASTLE, STIRLINGSHIRE

From its commanding rocky position, Stirling Castle has played
an important part in Scotland's history. More than 800 years
ago, King Alexander I died in the castle. But its heyday was
in the 13th and 14th centuries when it was prominent in
Scotland's struggle against the English: Sir William Wallace
recaptured it from the English in the 13th century; Edward I
snatched it back seven years later; ten years on it reverted to
Scottish hands when Bruce defeated Edward II at Bannockburn
in 1314. Later it became a favoured royal residence: James III
was born here; Mary Queen of Scots was brought to Stirling
Castle at the age of nine months and was crowned in the
Chapel Royal; her son, James VI, was christened in the Chapel
Royal and crowned in Stirling's Kirk of the Holy Rude.

Used as the headquarters of the Argyll and Sutherland
Highlanders, the castle is home to their museum.

▲ THIRLESTANE CASTLE, BERWICKSHIRE

Thirlestane Castle is regarded as one of the best preserved and
splendidly decorated historic buildings in Scotland. Originally a
13th-century fort at Lauder overlooking the River Leader, it was
rebuilt at the end of the 16th century as home of the Maitland
family who first came to Britain with William the Conqueror.
This building was in turn incorporated into a new design by
Sir William Bruce – Scotland's first professional architect – in
the 17th century. The present imposing red sandstone building
contains notable collections of paintings, furniture and china.
But its chief glory is its plasterwork by 'gentlemen modellers' –
craftsmen who worked on some of the most important
mansions in Britain, including Windsor Castle. Their work
is seen to best effect in Thirlestane's long drawing room.

The ghost of the 2nd Earl of Lauderdale, John Maitland
(1616–82), is said to haunt the castle.

TRAQUAIR HOUSE, PEEBLESSHIRE

With origins reaching back a thousand years, Traquair House is claimed to be the oldest inhabited house in Scotland. The tower, its oldest part, has been added to over the centuries. Traquair was once the home of William the Lion who held court here in 1209 and signed the charter that gave Glasgow its abbey lands. Twenty-seven Scottish and English monarchs have stayed at Traquair. The strongest royal association is with Mary Queen of Scots, who visited in 1566 with her baby son; relics on display in the house include the baby's crib, and Mary's rosary, crucifix and purse. The impressive gateway flanked by massive stone bears has been closed since 1745 and it is said that it will not be reopened until a Stuart ascends the throne.

The twentieth laird, the late Peter Constable Maxwell Stuart, did much to develop Traquair as a visitor attraction, including planting the substantial maze and re-opening the 18th-century brewhouse situated below the family chapel, brewing Traquair House ale for today's tourists thirsting after historical authenticity.